"Are we really us?
Love is all that we have"

AS LOVE MAY DO

RAAVI BAJAJ

PRABHAT PAPERBACKS

Published by
PRABHAT PAPERBACKS
An imprint of Prabhat Prakashan Pvt. Ltd.
4/19 Asaf Ali Road,
New Delhi-110 002 (INDIA)
e-mail: prabhatbooks@gmail.com

ISBN 978-93-5521-429-4
AS LOVE MAY DO
by Raavi Bajaj

Edition
First, 2023

Price
₹ 195 (Rupees One Hundred Ninety Five Only)

Printed at
Siddhi Press, Delhi

Foreword 1

Love is beautiful. There is no feeling better than being chosen. It has the power to make someone appreciate their imperfections and fall in love with themselves, the power to mend their broken parts and bless them with healing. Yet, people are afraid to love. They are afraid of giving it all to the wrong person. They are afraid of bearing the pain, which comes along with love.

"As Love May Do" is a collation of poems that make you feel so alive, so loved, yet so heartbroken at the same time. This book is not just words, it's rather a realization that there is always a first time for everything and so it is for love.

I am extremely delighted that Raavi has come up with this bracing anthology and I hope you have a wonderful time reading it. I feel proud, as an elder sister, to see her fulfill the dreams she carries in her eyes and reach new heights.

To loving and healing <3

– ***Rashi Bajaj***

Foreword 2

Love in any form is difficult to understand. And so it is difficult to understand life, which love makes up. We are all human beings strangled in our own web of atrocities, ranging from that one fight with our mom to missing that one friend who lives abroad, but there's one common bridge between existence and unconsciousness, that is the presence of love, that one feeling of being owned and loved by someone.

Articulating love in the form of a few words is difficult, even so difficult is to love and to accept love. And as a human being, it is perhaps, tiresome but the never ending efforts of giving love.

Being a writer, I understand the responsibility entrusted to engage the readers and successfully comprehend the meaning in this process. This whole idea of writing, editing, proofreading and the way it is polished brings out the entirety of these words.

The consistent efforts of Raavi Bajaj, in this process of accomplishment of As Love May Do, is a medium which aims to pen down the power of love and healing, at such a young and tender age.

Reading this book is entering into a place where one experiences every emotion when in love. We always talked about Raavi writing something different, and with this presentation, it is the apt definition of uniqueness.

Words are powerful, if used well. Through this anthology, words screech the meaning of love and the taste of it in life that lingers.

Hope you've a great time with this book, happy reading!

– Rishi Raj

Prologue

This seems a little scary as I can simply put. The entire 18 years of my life, are summed up. Hi everyone, whosoever is reading. I've no exact words to tell how much this work of two years mean to me, and I can't believe that it's officially published. I wrote this prologue verbally while going to bath, at the time I was about to sleep, while editing, I breathe writing and everything connected to it. I'm so blessed, I'd say that I'm actually getting the opportunity to let the world read my work. I know I'm not a very professional writer, I'm am an amateur artist who claims to feel emotional at the very thought of being praised. This book is not just a book, but a medium of words which carries my happiness and sincerity for eternity. There was a time when I thought writing a book is not my cup of tea, but eventually there were so many people who motivated me and were there at all times, to make me realise that I can and I will eventually pull off a book. I agree good and special things require time, and it did, and eventually after 2 years, I hand in you this because it's time you read it.

This world has quite a lot of people who don't believe in love because of their previous experiences and forget how loving they are as a person. The very presence of love in various different forms ranging from your parents, siblings and even things, like a toy tells how much you're actually connected to things and people. This book is not just an observation accounting for the relationships I've seen, but also the one I've been a part of. Infatuation or love does not matter, what matters are the amount of efforts and growth that you put in to ensure that it is a relationship built on the basis of two beings addressed as US and not Me. It's an amalgamation of you and your existence and coexistence with the other person. The world is made up of love, and so will it be in the future, because love is all that we have. :)

– Raavi Bajaj
As Love May Do

"To all the people who believe in the power of writing."

Contents

do you feel the same?

distance doesn't matter,
as long as you feel the same,
time starts to feel heavy,
when things aren't the same,
the going out together,
holding hands and sitting
on that bench,
the sun, pampering with its light,
the shy moon at night,
all the same,
But do you feel the same?
because things are different now,
we're different now,
same individuals but different times,
but some things remain the same,
you tell me,
Do you feel the same?

What does it mean to love?

you made me stronger,
the delicate stringency of being together,
the belongingness, which made us better.
it was a beautiful time, beautiful evenings,
with the strings attached to the heart,
the songs that we sing in love,
the miraculous feeling of knowing the unknown,
the way of approaching the truth of life with you,
and everything about you,
which made me happy, all this while,
all the things I longed for,
all the things I wanted to do with you,
you made me feel different.
you make me realize the meaning of love,
and everything connected to you.
you made me, you made me realize and understand
What does it mean to love?

Nauseated Life

I was feeling dead,
I didn't want to face the world I wanted to flee,
I was shattered and tears my soul shred.
Every day, every time I see you, consistently.
She died in my heart
Gave my life a new start
I realized she was no more
My heart was what she stole.
An elegant , enthralling girl
With eyes as beautiful as pearls
She was the love of my life
Without her , I can't imagine my life.

Life Goes On

Shattered into pieces,
was this red mass,
didn't know if I could breath anymore
I was muttering it's okay
it's okay to pretend as if everything is fine
but only the one with a broken heart
know how much it is okay
those memories cherished
when I remembered those dates,
those hugs, those days spent with my favorite mate
It was sad to rewind it all,
but I cannot pause,
after all it's life
we play it and it goes on and on
I felt hardly breathing
like a fish without water breathing
those breaths weighed a lot,
for in the last, last breaths in my air slot
I was going,
going to this beautiful heaven land,
for I wanted space,
space to let go of the hand of life

The Floret

You take a rose and kneel down,
But have you ever used to decorate the box,
The box containing shattered body parts,
And a broken heart.

we are "us"

the sun rays that coincide with the light,
the moon which misses its light,
the straight line which seems
complicated now,
I miss you, I realize it's different now.
the relationship we longed for,
the perfect amalgamation of
time and patience,
the world we made for us,
we two,
it's different,
i see you, i understand you,
I'm comfortable even when i'm in pjs with you,
I'm comfortable with you,
everything about you,
I'm glad you make me,
I'm glad "we make us."
I'm glad we are us.

Hold on

When you held me close that day,
With every breath, the descending distance,
As we inch closer,
And yet separate miles away,
We're inseparable demarcated souls,
That preach for love, because no one knows,
We might be different tomorrow,
Till then smile,
And press my heart till it hurts,
Till then hold on close,
Because it might be not be there,
We might not be there,
So hold on, and smile here.

You and Me

You and me are complicated,
Someway or somehow related,
I never get tired looking at you,
Talking to you,
You're the drops of the rain,
Your memory slides the tear,
As it does on the pane.

You and me

sometimes I think,
if it was meant for us,
it's alright if wasn't honey?,
but you've taught me a lot,
not to trust, time and again,
losing you made me find myself.

made my realize how much I loved you,
and how much I needed to love me,
because all this while,
What have you given? broken trust,
and a broken heart,
which'll always remember you,remember that.

You and Me

every night, i pretend to sleep,
silently wiping my face with the tears rolling down,
while reading Paper town,
and those days, moments, which I remember as I look down the street with it's light showering
it's brightness,
and my reflection in the mirror with loneliness,
reminds me of the sound of the rain that
drops on the ground,
my head spinning round,
and now what we're left with, are those memories cherished and the smiles,
and the car rides we used to have to travel miles.

You and Me

the world, place of atrocities,
and the search for love,
in the deep nights of melancholy,
and the bright skies too sunny,
what did I feel when I saw you?
perhaps, the moment when
I wanted to smile,
when I wanted to stop the time,
that time, you made me feel different,
the connection, ignited by your presence,
I miss you, realise your absence,
when you aren't there,
I stand here, all alone,
when the thought struck you're far away,
from the day when the sun shone,
and your sunlight, which left me confused,
it left me stunned,
Tell me, isn't that love?
When I saw you first, wasn't that love?

You and Memories

Have you ever been in love?

i don't know how it works,
all the strategies and tricks,
that you try to might them work,
honestly there's just one way to love,
and to give love,
that one bond of simplicity and trust,
conditioned to never rust,
because when in love,
everything might seem tough,
but when you're sure, everything seems simple enough.
Have you ever been in love?

You are something

What if I don't find?
The past nights have been blurry,
gone in confusion, I admit, they were heartbreaking and teary.
The stars have lost their shine,
and you're distant from being mine.
Because I know I can't hold onto someone and something for long,
they are bound to go,
no matter how much I want.
To be honest, what I need is not just you,
but the very essence of me which I've lost while searching for you.
But, what if I don't find?

That particular day

Wait
The wait is not for the one I lost,
but the wait who completes the one who is lost,
not the one who made me lost,
desperately waiting for this loss to heal,
to cope up with the missing zeal.

The Look

sometimes if things don't work out,
it's because they weren't meant to be
sometimes if you feel lonely,
hold the hand of life, and think,
about the sun, which seems lonely,
but it's light which ignites the entire sky.

think, and choose who you wanna be?
the sun or the star hidden in the moonlight

Descending hour

With the descending hours,
And less glistening stars,
A tear rolls in misery,
Tired, it came down pouring on the pane shivery,
Till now, I wonder it is just me missing you,
Or the moon also realises the need for those stars, two.

Glow

aesthetic lighting/the one window you look out of/the sky/moonlight
and reflection/time and again/i fall in love with you again/

the one time I heard your heartbeat,
the one time you felt so close,
the one it all happened,
It was this year. one time you felt mine,
felt old for time, nothing in hand, no worries to handle,
no things to hold onto,
you are there for the required all,
this year, I thank you for being mine,
waiting for the time, it has been beautiful,
you've been in my life.

The Daunting Silence

So far I haven't experienced the essence of love,
But that one expression,
When i see you and feel you,
When it's just the two of us,
When it's just we both,
We are engraving the moment for eternities,

Going to be remembered in infinities.
With the sun melting down,
the sky touching the ground,
descending every hour, every moment of the day,
those minutes, the seconds we pray.
for the melancholic figures hovering in the sky,
those untossed paper with the incomplete note, I sigh,
looking for that light in these times,
when everything seems, nauseating,
hopelessness hovers,
the rustling solidarity that persists,
it lays down, it sits.

As Love May Do

It'll take time, with the protocols,
for the flower to bloom, with the coexistence of weeds,
to sow the seeds,
of love, happiness and console, the one you're looking for.
in these tiring times,
these restless times,
of the deafening silence,
the beauty of the flower,
that essence of being bloomed,
in these situations not so smooth.
What remains is the meaning of this existence,
that feeling intense,
which is consistent for a long time,
find yourself, in these times.
you're your own strength and might,
see yourself and value your sight.

The Rustling solidarity

The candles are all lit,
Where they stand at the end of the table,
Remember the time when it was all stable,
I stood witnessing all memories washing down the pane,
Standing alone amidst the lane,
Scrutinised, nauseated and yelling in pain.
I wish for the togetherness, those promises we did to each other,
Sweared on our mothers,
This silence and the state of tranquillity,
Lay there in shatters of serenity.

You're awaited

It's been so long,
we've have been struck for so much time,
i know this might not be the right place,
but know this, this is right for you to know
I couldn't gather up courage to tell you
that i miss you and somehow you are in my dreams.
I know this year,
this year, has been tough and separated the two of us,
I know agreeing is a must,
but admit that we've been distant.
Okay, yes, I saw you last year,
when I hugged you, and we laughed our way through,
and as usual, I knew we would meet soon,
life, alas, knew the truth.
Life knew the truth,
that it's not for a month,
but for a year, I couldn't see you.
Video calls, zoom were our favourites,
and not meeting a dream.
After 12 months, when I see you,
today, when I see you,
you are still that person,
that beautiful sunshine, though it obstructs my sight,
but it is serene to see that light.
I love you!

It's okay

It's okay to fall down,
crouch and cry,
but you should never stop trying
The road to success,
is not fleeing
striving hard and falling
is a part worth seeing
It's okay if you can't be happy all the same,
It's okay to have bad days,
It's better you accept them as they lay
It's okay to smile when you want to,
be yourself wherever you wish to,
know that you're one of a kind,
and ideas that cook up only in your mind
It's okay to be there for someone every time,
though they don't validate you much,
it doesn't care much,
you are happy, that's the matter.
It's okay to fall apart,
but it's okay to get back too,
no matter how many times you fall,
cry, bitch, be sad, get mad,
where ever you're being sent to,
know that you're going to be successful too.

One chance

I know it might have happened,
But do you regret it?
Do you regret those glistening stars,
Those walks beneath the moon which slid its shadow,
That road which was too narrow,
Those cold hands of mine,
Which you held onto, when we crossed the road,
One chance, maybe? Would you come with me,
Would you come again to experience the cold night,
To experience the thirst of your sight,
What you've missed, what your soul missed,
Going there exactly where I shove those marks on my wrist.
One chance, would you come with me?

Hear myself

I couldn't hear myself out,
As expected, I thought mine would last long,
I looked at you and thought you're the one,
You're like none.
I see you, standing with the broken chain in your hand,
The broken trust of the two of us,
And you still like to be the one?
I tried till I couldn't,
I stood till I couldn't,
I waited for you till I could stand straight,
In the end, I was in dilemma,
Couldn't hear myself, my state.

The lasts

Your scent lingers,
Your presence stays,
You can come as and when you may,
I stand in the long queue of love,
Waiting for that day, when will someone stay?
When someone will wait for me,
When someone will see me,
As I saw you once,
I picture the scenario, where we stood long lost in the streetlights,
Not just once, but in my dream, I dream about you tons.

One more time

One last time,
These candles are waiting to lit,
They are tired of this melancholy darkness,
The figures hovering high,
With me staring at the windows,
With the moon, which sigh,
Waiting for you,
In the deep thoughts,
I lay awake at night,
Wishing for that one more time.

Torn Teenager

The teenager torn and confused wondered,
Fumbled and suffered,
Sometimes it's hard to understand ,
Who you are and what is this love mad?
The mannequin stood still,
After taking those pills,
Aghast, tired, and at the threshold,
Superficial world is extremely bold.
They couldn't understand what the illusion love carried,
They look at the couple who was getting married,
Wondered if love makes the heart beat,
A bliss or a beauty for thousands to meet?

Those days

Those starting days were good, right?
when we used to cut the call at 3 am
my maa thinking I'm asleep,
and would rush inside and peep,
if she's sleeping or awake for me.
I remember telling you each thing,
about me, my friends, my past,
I thought this was going to be permanent, but well, it didn't last,
it didn't last so long,
I kept looking at the clock,
looking at the sky outside when I'll go out with you next time.
The next time i thought would be after the virus felt a little less,
and there was less stress,
I would go out and engulf in the warm hug,
I woke up and saw the morning as my sister tug
yes, I dreamed about you that night,
thinking this couldn't be true right?
now that you're gone, with tangled fights and spaces,
with me stuck in this labyrinth, this maze.
Last thing I pray for you as I write this,
if you know this, you're being missed,
but the destiny wasn't in our hands,
let go separate in our lands.

Will you?

Before anything you're yours,
even the melancholy stars shine bright,
obstructing the sight,
full in fright, and that terrible phobia
What if you love nyctophilia?
you're yours and mine,
Never in an eternity, would those craving eyes deny,
always and forever you'll be with me,
beneath the stars,
where the shadows run away,
in envy and rival,
you're still struggling, I sense that.
Once, in a lifetime, I want you to give me a chance,
i don't care if it's the first or last,
just one thing,
Would you come with me?
Far behind the stories of saudade,
you and I lay, on those windy days,
with the windows down,
you waving out, happy, and proud.
This time, I promise you,
Those cosmogyral nights,
I long for them,
the lasts that lingered,
they tag along in my memory,
because you're tough to let go.

For you, I might be that simplest of curtains that you draw,
and hide the sunlight that dropped in,
for me, you're those rays, who despite my longing to let go,
is stuck there, rigid, my thoughts flew
I flew, out of this imagination,
because that one chance, I fear,
you'll give that to me,
Will you?

May not be perfect

The crescent moon,
I stare long, long, as time flies by,
that rising ball of energy rises,
and I realize it's morning,
never knew how eyes weren't tired
I look along the lines of those drops,
that follow, my way, to this height,
I'm in fear and fright,
I don't know how I'm.
This may not be the perfect time but honestly,
I know I want to tell you,
I'm like you, but I'm not too.
I want to be with you, but I'm scared,
long ago, I stared,
you, and that moon,
which was shy in front of you,
i would stick next to you,
those exultant memories fly by,
I'm swarmed with questions,
As well, feel you, that you're not present,
the feeling of lacuna,
i know i may not be perfect,
i know I've a defect,
that i love you,
which may not be perfect.

Can't help falling

The light falls in,
Unravels the glistening light,
With the salty tears on my glasses that roll down,
In despair, at this point, I can't fight.
I believed in the gaiety of my laughter,
When the sky bowed to me,
The birds sang,
The blue sky wasn't blue,
But like those blush cheeks of mine,
The pink sky shined.
I believed in love,
Never knew how it would get through,
Never planned my life to get this much screwed,
The scented candles wait,
For the fire to ignite,
Highlighted it's quietude,
The conflicting moods,
I can't understand on my own.
The dust veiled pages of my notebook,
Hooked in the air,
Those writings are of no use anymore,
As I stare. My voice is shaking,
I can't speak, my thoughts are weaving.
Into that one thing I believed in when I saw you before,
I can't help falling in love, once more.

There might be days

There might be days
you might want to cry,
because that day wasn't the day you expected,
that atrocious ignited fire,
to roar, to shout,
yell, signals, please come back.
that one flower lays restless.
The perfect sunshine was there,
every two and three, roots were watered,
the soil was damp enough,
but wasn't damp enough for everyone to see.
I waited for a long time,
waving, swinging, enjoying from time to time,
destiny wasn't my friend,
I had to go, I knew, near was my end.
the multi-dimensional wall i was embedded in,
i knew i didn't commit a sin,
Why was I even in it?
I longed to go out for the sun to pour over my petals,
it cried aloud, when one of the siblings were plucked,
it didn't end me being me, that one long flower i wanted to be.
I bloomed into a flower that can't be bloomed,
in a dream that can't come true.
In the end, it was the last breath i took,
standing by there, on the hook,
i sighed and withdrew,
my roots and stick,
I knew I wasn't the lucky pick.

I know

I know I shouldn't have fallen in this trap of love,
The atrocious struggling light,
Which keeps me up every night,
Wondering about you being mine.
It's a different kind of feeling, I know,
Thank you for making me feel that,
But it's been five years lad,
It's not one of those fantasies and dreams,
Every night, my tears screech me to sleep,
It is full of nightmares and screams,
I wonder, if I was wrong,
Or are the actions evoked by destiny strong?
I swear I had the best time of my life,
enjoying and being happy and not survive,
had I known life would be this brutal,
And love so scrutinised subtle,
I doubt if I'll be the same person,
who used to yearn for love at one point,
but I'm grateful to you for teaching me that way,
of knowing unknowingly and staying away.
I know you are the one you taught me,
Thank you for doing so.

Daunting Eyes

I swear loving from a distance hurts,
But when I see you from close, my destiny mutters
The way you look at me,
Those daunting eyes of being close,
Being in that one love dose,
When we're inclined towards each other,
Yet be distant.
I thought love seemed easy,
But that look of care and comfort,
I'm shy to even let go,
And think about the worst, what if I leave you?
I can't seem to be in terms of breaking you,
Tearing you apart,
When you needed me, at any time, any hour,
This life is unfair and a race of struggle showers.

My life

Engulfed in this pool of love,
As they say, it is tough,
The moment of being in love,
Is fearful to play with,
Those pillows hit hard, my eyes itch,
Been crying all night,
For that one person who I am not even sure if he's right?
Love made me blind,
So did his mysterious eyes, with those warm hugs,
I tug behind,
I care for him more than I do for myself,
He doesn't care for me now,than himself,
And that time I realize I was wrong,
That hit me hard, but hit me strong,
To value myself over some random guy,
Who I thought was my world, and my life.

The atrocities

The atrocities in my mind,
Were not just those entangled love stories,
Those sleepless nights what would happen,
If you were in love?
It might be difficult to even remember beneath those shrieking tired eyes,
Looking out for you to be mine, alas the day , I hope
I hope, isn't too far to reach.

Would you come with me?

The imperfect perfect crescent moon,
i look over, and yearn for your touch,
which left too soon,
please, can you come once?
this lifetime is incomplete without you,
come here for a night or two,
know that this is not done,
I miss you every day, tons.
Hey, would you come with me?
once and for all,
we'll meet and catch up,
talk out all things we couldn't,
all things left to tell,
i want to tell you, at night, i yell,
when I miss you,
and realized how much I loved you.
One last time,
would you come with me?.

I stare

And behind those entrapped
Circles of melancholy light,
And sleepless nights,
I sleep in fright,
Thinking about that sight,
When I saw you walking up,
The stairs,
The stars envy your glare,
Astound, I stood as I stared.

Still lay

The whistling songs of the nature,
and the way he whispers,
shimmers and rises in the dry land,
hazy is the vision covered with sand.

That day the flower which was gifted,
still lay in the river of plasma,
undergoing was the trauma and uncertainty,
I couldn't decide whom to pity.

I walked down, and wondered which song to play,
the guitar lay there waiting,
with the beauties whispering in silence,
feared to believe the bitter violence.

Those marks lay and shine in the sunlight,
i wondered about change,
when and where, it might,
might bring a change in you,
to save a life or two.

What is Love?

"Love" is that beautiful silence which once enlightened roars like a fire. It's not exactly a chapter of life, but what exactly makes up life. That scorching sun in the eyes, those whispering winds kissing the plants, isn't that love too? We've grown to beings in this manipulative world, not knowing that love is what one looks up to. that That essence of making the smile last for a while, hearing yourself out, the presence of love is what makes up you as a person, when in love. Just like you can't skip a chapter or phase of your life, love is inevitable that one bridge exists between you and oblivion. That one star which shines with your inner beauty and that one light you look up to when you're happy,
IN LOVE.

That night

One blurry night,
I do remember how you looked before you told me you were going out,
randomly I turned around and found you awake,
there, in the middle crying,
tired and muffled accompanied by uncomfort.
I didn't know what you were doing that night,
I woke up to your sound,
I turned out to look towards you,
and you hastily slept that blurry night
The next night you told me that you were not okay,
I held you beside me,
hugged you, and told you,
hey it's fine to not be okay,
it's fine to be lost sometimes,
the world is not perfect and you don't have to be perfect too,
you're you,
maintain that,
Know that I'm here to hold you,
Wherever and whenever you go wrong.

that faded memory

those restless nights,
whispering things which were right,
that little touch, we yearned for,
Is it missing or we left it?
Things aren't what we promised for,
underneath the filtered light,
the moon too weak to remember,
but those words scream out aloud

It's been long since we talked,
that last night we met,
seems like a thousand years,
honey, it's just what I've have,
and it has left me in tears.
you might have moved on, but
it's difficult to forget you, your smile and the touch,
it still haunts me,
scares me of that one night full of mystery,
that one faded memory.

I wonder

I've always wondered,
in the deep dwellings of the minds of society,
and the candle that flickers in the dark,
aren't they the same? They fiddle and highlight or darken as per their need,
can be beautiful or a weed,
in the obstruction of the beautiful being,
that you were once, if you see.
If you see through the cruel eyes,
in the rough times,
it darkens and leaves those purple marks on the paper,
The paper recklessly restless, cannot do anything, even straighten.
The fragile conditions of the beautiful paper,
is crumbled and thrown away,
legs are held, to stop them from swaying away.

Scratching must

The cacographist,
Lost in the lust,
Laid down as he must,
With scratching of the relief, exploring the bewildering trust.

You're the one

Those red crystal lies,
sharp, daring beautiful eyes,
in the thorny beautiful lie,
you're that one in my life.
it's hard to draw the curtains when you know everything is absolutely wrong,
handle the beauty with the flaws,
with each descending hour,
you're the one I admire my star,
your ways, taste, smile, all will be mine,
share one part of your life.
a part where you are you and I'm who I'm,
the stars envy your shine,
your resting palm, that ooze the beauty of the night,
testing me to stay and a trial on my might.
i know you are more than i could ever have deserved,
late at night, i wondered and poured, on the thought that kept me awake,
if that night, you'd stay when remains none,
to know if you're the one.

Silent silences

These candles with the flickering lights,
Yearning for the bright sight,
The bewildering trust,
Lays no rest, even in the deepest nights,
It screams and shouts the fears,
Forcing the salty tears,
To flow down, shatter and break the silence,
The silent voice breaking the violence.

One night

That one particular night,
When being lost, what is wrong or right,
Seeing in that catastrophic space,
Stuck in the labyrinth maze,
That night called for that one moment to reach,
In the years to come,
for the relationship to preach,
And celebrate
You and Me.

The Calamitous Peace

Never thought of actually experimenting serenity,
of being doomed for an eternity,
The essence of lifting each other up at all times,
And becoming us to you're mine.
The existence asks for a lot,
It is a triumph disaster,
Like a flickering light, dark and bright,
Secluded from the feeling to me,
To become a togetherness of we.

It's not easy to touch the intimacy of the world,
Which revolves around, as you stand stun,
It's not easy to maintain peace with yourself,
When you've found the one,
And that matters,
Which changes the entirety of the feelings you possess,
Perceiving yourself as a blessing,
And not in distress.

The Eternal Love

The shrieking shatters in distress,
The melancholy figures evoke a mess,
You've time to evaluate me for yourself,
No matter how tough it is,
I'm here and it won't change ever,
Know that it's fine to take your time,
I'll wait for you,
For your eternal love,
Throughout my life.

Lost love

The scent lingered,
Tackled beneath the skin you once touched,
Within the vicinity of your body,
That sweet essence of your presence is missing,
Looking for in the dark lost night,
That flickering dim light,
of the love that we lost that shone bright.

Don't know how

I didn't know how,
It feels to be in love,
To be with a person in proximity,
Experience calmness and serenity,
Until I saw you,
Back then

Didn't know, it was this magical,
Those evoking images which were mystical,
Serene and lovingly beautiful,
Those memories provoke and trigger now,
Forces me to shatter and erase the evidence of us,
Were we together in this,
Were we even really us?

Melancholy happiness

Never thought I'd say this,
But you're not here anymore,
The word promise aches my heart out,
Because anyways it's broken right?
What you said,
Wasn't true,
Those things weren't meant,
Time was spent,
Expecting the happily ever after.

You're different

The way she went made me feel a breeze of consciousness. "You are somebody I'd like to be with." I'd never say that. But she is different . My "you and me" as they say, "Nothing of this sort will ever melt me" those cliché words and suspicion are not my thing.

But today, when I saw her, I believed in the barbaric yet beautiful "you and me."

Waiting

I crouched down,
in the dark,
in despair, going dizzy,
I could not get up,
strangled I was in those crazy locks.
My love for you hasn't changed,
Somehow you act strange,
the feeling of being lost,
is common nowadays, around as I toss.
I can't guess why we aren't cool,
Could you speak and tell me why I am considered a tool?
I'm writing this to you,
to know that I haven't stopped caring,
your choice, but I'll wait for you ,
wait for you, looking at the sky,
Waiting for the stars to continue staring.

Delicate mass

A crack on a glass
On a red delicate mass,
Shattered into pieces lay crying
Never going to get back how much you try.

Finally

Finally the time had come,
For the darkness was taken over,
My happiness had finally taken off
Not that I've done something
Or I've found someone,
It's a different kind of feeling,
A feeling of liberty and getting free from anxiety
It feels fresh today not because somebody has done black magic on me,
But because I've learnt to enjoy
Enjoy with what I have
And not carrying the guilt of not saying hi to someone I know
I'm carefree, fragile and more or less happy in life,
Today, I forget you
And vanish everything we had.

Like the moon

Like the moon,
You make my heart skip a beat at noon,
The way your reflection is filtered,
Bent, scattered is my heart and soul,
Makes me believe in love again.

Dark

In the dark spheres of night,
With the melancholy figures hovering,
The mind deviates and nothing seems right,
Nothing seems right because he is missing..

Light

the blanket/moon/sunlight/sleep/the missing light/you (ofcourse).

the blanket seems warm today, just like I used to feel warm in your arms, the place I called mine. the sun is out, it's 5 am, and i don't know i can't sleep, i keep looking out across the window, and sense the fight between the moon and the sun. the moon hides away behind the sun's light, just like the scars which scream silently in the morning. i yearn for you, look for you, search for you, but you're probably not there because it's not meant to be. you're not there, because you were never there. :(

Those little attempts

Never exactly realized the efforts,
Did you do any?
When those tears,
Roll down after years,
You remember one thing,
Which you missed, that night in that blink,
Which vanished with all memories,
What if you tried a little more?

Are we us?

Deep down, every night,
This thought occurs to me,
As the star see,
And glare at the pointless me,
Staring longingly at the moon,
My life seems tough,
It wonders, is somebody there whom I can call my own,
Somebody I can rely on,
That particular one, makes me remember of you,
And our tangled mess,
Are we really us?

That's how it is

Don't you think love is unfair, like life,
Certainly uncertain,
No yes no no, just disappearing in thin air,
As and when it seems as a choice,
For once, I thought, us to be somewhat unmoving,
Turns out, we're in an illusion,
Of whatever the life puts forward,
The love is same too,
We're same too for us,
But that's how it is, as they say.

Us

I never cared to think about the transition from we to us,
till the time we got separated,
all alone in that stranded mind of mine,
all scattered, which once used to shine,
I look across, and see,
the incomplete you and me?

A chance

Long along the lines that led me to the monotonous me,
those shatters of mirror that scream,
which one had my vision with dreams,
How and when did this happen?
I'd never imagined to depart from us to you and me,
all day long, I sense the intensity when I wish to flee,
and I can't, cannot imagine a world without "we".
It's difficult to understand what we promised,
because we never tried,
never-ending vicious cycles of distress,
those painful nights,
sitting in fright,
What if you had given "us" a chance?

For you

I did everything I could do possibly,
For the result of this vicious cycle,
Of pain that you pretended to care for,
It's been so long, move on,
Because no matter how much you've hurt me,
It's going to come back to you,
What did you to me,
For you.

Is it really?

All the promises we made,
Was a waste,
That nauseated thought of being deadly alive,
Didn't know how you could even survive?
They said I cared too much,
And you pretended to care too much,
Never knew if I wrong to believe them or you,
Because I couldn't solve this entangled mystery,
Is it really?

Fiddling thoughts

The pages of my journal haunt me with our memories,
When you blessed those pages with your love and touch,
Do they miss it or do I miss it so much?
Days have passed, with those missing memories,
Which once belonged to us,
I know it is not easy for you to belong to me again,
Because what's once broken, can't be repaired with one,
Requires the two broken joints, to come together,
With empathy, to give love to someone else too.

at 3 am

at 3:00 am,
the melancholy figures shine,
and those beautiful memories that lay at the back of my mind,
wondered when you were mine?

I walked down the aisle,
enjoying the tap on stepping on each tile,
looked up and sighed,
tired and torn, sad and risky
were the ocean of tears tied, asking when they can come dried?

I walked towards the park, with those little drops splashing,
with my face I could see in it's reflections,
this rain, I remember, which drowned our good memories,
now screeched with screams and those happy dreams.

I remember we meeting on this particular slide,
you sitting on the damp side,
for me to not get a scold from my mother,
you dropped the warm blazer on my shoulder and whispered,
to be with me by my side, wherever it was,
to be with me at all times.

Months passed in the beauty of our fantasies,
cute gifts and meeting each other were a must,
as I pass by that particular rock, dusty and engrossed in mud,
you standing on that to click a picture with me, captioned as stud.

Today when I look by,
I sigh and look down,
Look at the footprints of our feet where we stood at exactly 8:00 pm,
where we stood and wished the last thing,
To stay beautiful and never let those drops come out that stand on the brink.

Fear

The constant fear kills me from inside,
some days it's scary,
how will our lives be, if we aren't together,
Love haunts me, and shatters those memories,
those promises we made once,
which makes me remember the constant fear of losing you, love.

Our end

Can't get over the thought of getting lost,
To wander alone in the dark shades of night,
Which was once filled by the smudge of the both colors,
Who needed time to merge,
To mix together for a surge,
And upliftment in happiness and those moments to have an end,
But before that,
Are we sure of our end? Which is smudging now,
And departing with the flow of water,
Or the irresistible end which is going to stand by all the time.

Belief

The lost belief in the mist of love,
Once appeared strong with prominent detail,
Lost it's shine nurturing the other figures,
Now looked gray and pale,
This atrocity of the lost senses in hail,
The moon will shine bright again,
Once it has healed from the pain of the shooting star,
That hit the ground, at night,
With the lost strength and might.

I wonder

And I wonder if the stars envied that night,
because of the fragile fright,
we sensed that night.
The moon disappeared behind the melancholy figures,
which yearned for the colors to merge,
with the outward beauty of white color,
Was it beautiful inside too?
I was difficult to keep track of that sight,
which I write with sigh,
was and always remain the best night,
when I tried..

The memory

The distant memory,
Of falling and meeting under that particular spot,
With the sun scorching over the top,
You walking towards with the glass in your hand,
Now it seems missing, I suppose you're glad,
You walk this time too,
With the glass over the other table,
To promise that new one, to be with her at all times,
No matter what hour, what time.

This, you did this once to me,
Engulfed in deep sorrow, I pity myself,
For trusting with my soul,
What did you do,
Walked away, tearing apart, circling around a hole.
That glass that day,
Now lays alone with the shadow of the sun from above ,
It is broken and shattered,
With the haunted flashbacks blurry,
Of our special memory.

Failed to understand

Love is all about those strangled rectified hierarchies that hypocrisy craves. It's not just an unfair mode of distraction and pretending to be intimate, it's a facade that people put up because they mistook the meaning of love. They understand love as that pleasure seeking relationship which is based on the exchange of materialism, and not feelings. This closeness of two people is not because they feel something, but they can just term themselves to be in LOVE. Love is a complicated whole, which requires understanding between two beings to nurture and grow with each other. It requires time, space to grow into a beautiful bond they didn't even think of.

Scorching sun

The sun comes by,
to smell the scent, when you first came by,
tangled in the tears which drops in it's sunshine,
once, when I called you mine,
Once it used to be us,
down it goes and glows along the street,
expecting an unexpected meet.

Will you be you?

Deep down, as they say, everything that you do comes with a fear,
This time, I've a fear of losing you,
When it'll be no, us, and no one to call mine,
That would be so helpless,
All the promises we've done to each other,
Of staying with each at all times,
Being a helping hand, in all the chores,
And me falling for you more,
Day by day,
Just don't disappear when I need you,
Any day, when the moon doesn't shed enough light,
I'll need you to guide me then,
Meddle in, to do the work with hands two,
In that situation, will you step forward,
Will you be you?

Sight

That particular sight,
with the light interfering between us,
I thought it was temporary,
didn't know would be accompanied with melancholy figures,
with the hail and rain,
ruining our moment,
was it for the good,
that we didn't get to meet?
because if we had, these would have been the dreadful sight
with tears,
that I feared.

Long night

The long night,
I was waiting for it to pass,
it lasted a while,
not knowing how will I act in the morning in a fuss,
with you in my dreams last night,
I know it wasn't right,
because it has been broken once,
don't want to take the risk again,
it's gone, but there's still a stain.

You're the one

Walking across the room,
you're the one for whom I stop,
with the sunlight pouring,
you're the one for whom I let it fall in my eyes,
with the rain falling down the pane,
you're the one for whom, I let it down, to enjoy the sound,
you're the one for whom I've been waiting,
now that you're in reach,
Are you even here?

For

in the deep intricacies of mind,
when the sight isn't inclined,
where the mind continues to think,
over and over without a blink,
and the heart and the game of steal,
one question that troubles the complexities is why do we feel?
feelings, perhaps, the most prominent ways of expression,
running away from complications,
Do you think it is a justification?
justification for the world to adjust in,
for the same things to feel,
for the same reason to be,
for the same person to be with,
Why do you think we feel and think?

You're real

You're the real example of love,
that stream of consciousness,
intertwined, in our touches,
and those moments of affection,
you're the real one,
that person,
whom I call mine.

Do you?

Do you understand me,
and that love which we shared,
do you remember,
that day we met and smiled at each other,
those eyes which lie,
that they have forgotten that love,
but I'm sure, it's not the eyes that matter,
it's you, who is afraid to admit,
that the love is inevitable,
and understand that it's difficult to stop yourself,
do you, don't you?

Choice

the choice of you staying more,
the choice of you being mine for long,
the choice of pulling over and not vanishing when you wanted,
the choice of being us,
the choice of being connected,
and you choosing me, for once?

Eyes said

The last meeting of us,
in the backyard when we left each other,
and what we did , “breakup”
that night, the eyes said,
they deny this reality and I wonder why,
why can’t the reality agree,
to being us, to what the eyes said.

Come closer

The world is entrapped in a bubble,
of those sorrows that are hidden behind the happiness,
those vows of trust and belief,
that break, if two beings don't dwell in the relationship,
but you and me are different,
two beings who are in control of ourselves,
and what's to be done, if any obstruction comes,
pop that bubble,
come closer,
give the warmth needed to warm the fire down.

The hidden love

The hidden love,
behind the chains of trust that have rusted,
behind the clouds of fiddling thoughts,
that keep me awake,
even when I know you're pretending to sleep,
that hidden love of ours,
find each other awake,
as we turn to see if the other person has slept or not.

The last time

The last time we saw each other,
When our lips were silent,
No external speech,
Just the mind hovering the little thought,
Is it what I got? In the end,
It's just me,
And I'm happy with it,
And have this hope consistent in my mind,
And brain
Till we depart,
That you're okay too.

It's fine

It’s fine if you leave now,
because i know what we really meant,
I know what I mean to myself,
and the time I lost you, because I lost myself.
This is a constant fear of losing,
but what’s worse than losing myself.

Whatever

Whatever has happened,
has happened,
but it's time to let go and love too,
it's time to know that love is important,
but so is attention and peace to yourself.
And it's not difficult after what happened,
with you and me,
Whatever happened, happened for our good..

For you

It's long past those nights,
those stressful nights, and sleeping in fright,
we don't know the value of something till someone disrupts you and that something,
which you yearned for, remembering that someone,
and it's a long time,
me yearning and willing for you, your touch,
but it's a little love to me now,
those apologies to regret the guilt I've now,
when I followed throughout the night,
and didn't care about the weak reflection of mine, and those blindness ways, when I followed
but a letter to me,
for this special night,
for not giving much attention to someone, never
for you, my love, a thousand times over. :)

Timestamp

1:58am it's been raining outside for the past ten hours. there's a new freshness in plants and the environment is smiling today, it's getting washed away and clean devoid of dust.

2:00am i wonder when it'll stop raining. the panes are all wet and drops prickle on my skin as I go outside with the warm coffee in the flask i got gifted on a rainy evening like today's.

2:15am it seems distant to even plug in earphones and listen to our "rainy day song." that song, amalgamation of words and rhythm, doesn't match our sound relationship.

2:30am weather is getting a little better. the sound of raindrops is descending and my coffee is nearly finished.

2:45am i stand up to keep the coffee flask on the bedside table and turn off the lamp. the essence of hot light is felt and i feel warm.

3:00am too late for my cognitive abilities to function properly. i changed into my pajamas, and the mickey mouse t-shirt. As I turn, i hear a thunderstorm and the warning of a sleepless night.

4:00am i woke up, because i couldn't sleep. I turn onto different sides,but there's no sign of fatigue and i stay there, lying awake.

6:00am i hear the birds chirping, witness the rising sun's rays and sleep in my eyes. With a sleepy head, i rest my head and doze off.

You

The pen rests on the desk,
with the fiddling thoughts and mess,
in the mind, which affects me everyday.
Those melancholic figures hover,
and deep down I miss those times,
when going out wasn't a sin,
when smiling was common,
and when I could recognize myself as me,
because I was present at that time.
Even in the dark times,
just as i was about to give up,
that one ray, that struck out, from the figures,
shone out too bright,
obstructing the sight,
and that optimism will spill out.

What matters is you,
and that you've to be there for yourself more than being there for others.
Don't yearn for that hand to heal,
when you know that you yourself can heal yourself,
and you, need to realise your own worth,
and the light, within you, needs to spread out,
out to the world,
and in these times,
you help yourself to help others.

Breath

The gushing of the wind,
remembering deep down the melancholic figures hovering,
empowering the shining light,
the breeze went by,
with the reminiscences of the past.
Difficult to let go,
and the nauseated fiddling thoughts,
makes the chances of survival negligible.
The rage of thinking about those things,
how loud breaths are prominent,
What if we become happy for a moment?
and forget it underneath.
We don't comprehend properly the concept of the gushing breeze,
the wind and sound of the chirpy creatures,
the moment of being happy,
and realising what is our breath?

We don't understand how it goes slightly high,
or low according to us,
and we blame our destinies and supreme power for actions,
when it is us, whose existence is in this illusion,
this bubble of dreams, and aspirations,
all the notions,
which can come true with a breath, if controlled,
and not the breath controlling us,
because at the end of the day,
it's us and we need to carve our own way,
till the end day, of death,
question yourself what is breath?.

Favourite poem

The Favourite flow of words,
in the tangled confusing string that carries a meaning,
is not what is a favourite poem.
Those words which do not make you cry,
but makes you remember of those facades,
and times when you weren't you yourself,
and when you needed yourself.

Those words, and rhyme,
are not what it shines,
it isn't about those glimmery stars,
which wait in anticipation, and are tired of looking ,
yearning out for the moon,
rather the power and strength,
illuminated by the stars to light up the moon,
and not to end so soon.

The favourite lines,
which are not related yet are not distinct,
and seem familiar to me,
and those lines even though,
don't meet at a point,
are looking out for a meaning,
for those words wait,
to be tangled in the rope of love,
and the strength of the universe.

What is a poem?

The word screech for help,
the ink prints them furiously,
they don't tend to go along with each other,
but somehow they rhyme and mutter,
they are tired of screaming.
Fiddling thoughts and noting them down,
in a mystical way,
exploring each aspect of the day,
never figured out how it all went,
but it's a gift sent.
The art is different and special,
requires vigilance and tolerance,
can be about happiness and mess,
the presence of you embedded in the creation,
makes it special for the readers.
The timing is not a coincidence,
it can be a result of resistance,
but those thoughts and words won't leave you,
might make you stronger too.
I rest my head on the ink,
which waits for the words to be penned down,
With the question to express the gem,
What is actually a poem?

This is life

Fear steps up,
Throws you into dark,
It's risky, torn and naive,
Remember this is what is Life.

It maybe good one day,
The other day it throws you in melancholy,
It decides to reside in and stay all night,
Remember this is what is Life.

The flame of ego will burst,
The desire to go out, yell, a strong thirst,
But tell that you're a warrior right?
Remember this is what is Life.

It's easy to go out and rant,
It's okay for some days to be sad,
It will teach you to struggle a ton,
Remember this is what is Life my son.

You and I

the melancholic night,
my mind stranded in your thought,
the one light i was looking out, for you,
in the deep intricacies of mind,
looking for that one chance,
and one moment, for you to be mine,
which remains incomplete,
you and I are complementary, yet different,
you and I make a beautiful duo,
but are you even mine right now?
we're not sure, yet need each other <3

I remember

I remember that screeching of the wheels,
when you used to come home,
that running, muffling through the curtains,
going out and finding you hiding in the pane,
coming while tiptoeing, pretending to be in pain.

I remember you coming out immediately,
hearing me in pain,
I used to laugh supposedly, knowing it was just a game.
Those pictures were a bundle of joy and freedom,
and now, we go out seldom

I remember you being the doctor,
In the doctor doctor game,
Mother used to shove household chores to you,
and thought that was lame,
you told me to play with my children and I realise this today.

I remember now looking down to those albums,
going down town to buy the Johnson talcums,
which I use them on my children,
and give them bundles of what I got, love and affection.

I remember, Dad,
you were my star and now are till,
I remember going out in your hands,
I do it with my children, with your touch,
Till eternity, I'm going to remember those memories,
I'm going to give them these memories.

Be mine?

Strangled and torn,
That feeling i had worn,
for a very long time,
Fiddling thoughts in between I strived
I looked and smiled by,
wondering when will this be mine?
The happiness and joy with time
came autonomously without any help,
I cry, yelp, shout
but they tell me, you're not worth, just shut your mouth.
I know i have been quiet all this while ,
lost in my way, my lifestyle,
I've been torn and stuck in between
never knew life would be this mean.
but i know for this fact, that sun comes out slow,
it's okay to feel silent and low,
Just smile your way through all this while,
make sure you live and not survive in this life.

She

Don't go out at night" is what girls get to hear,
with each descending hour, they shed tears,
with each person going against the good,
How can one expect to reach motherhood?
with the ongoing voicing of opinions,
there's no equality within anyone,
boys are superior, considered to be superior,
there she stands with the cloth over her head, in front of the mirror,
and wonder about those wrists on her hand,
Does she feel pity for herself or her destiny?
I say, get up and help her today,
she's not rigid, she's not made up of clay,
know that she is enough, who she is,
make her strong, and fear her if she is pissed.
support her in every work,
don't stalk her or glare at her when she is at work,
she's beautiful and serene like the woods and the tree,
don't forget her and make her a "She.

I Fail

That ooze of blood,
I tell you, it's not easy son,
those twisted strangled lies,
within those uncanny eyes.

I fail to be the person I used to be,
i fail to say that optimism lives across the sea,
far, far away from the land,
No matter what I want, it's difficult my lad.

I try to protect her from rays,
there are rough bad days,
with shifting of legs, uneasy sleep,
and the shuffling of her huge eyes, tired to weep

Yet her she lies in the darkness,
Traumatised and pushed repeatedly,
into the vicious cycle of hatred and madness,
With an ooze of blood, she sleeps forever timidly.

the day

Well, the story is kind of complicated,
I was kind of devastated,
so were those lines across my wrist,
those stars I made, while watching the mist.

The page my vision rested on,
stopped for a while
as I lay uneasy on my bed last night,

I wondered about the first pile.
The first pile of those notebooks,
and as I open my secret diary,
at the end page,
the last page says, shush it's private.

The whistling songs of nature,
that picture of a guitar that lay
and the way he whispered
all came back in a flashback,
shimmered and rises in the dry land,
hazy is the vision covered with sand.

That special day,
when the flower was gifted,
still lay in the river of plasma,

undergoing was the trauma and uncertainty,
I couldn't decide whom to pity,
is evident in the picture.
I walked down, and wondered which song to play,
the guitar lay there waiting,
with the beauties whispering in silence,
feared to believe the bitter violence.

Those marks lay and shine in the sunlight,
I wondered about change,
when and where it might,
might bring a change in you,
to save a life or two.

I realized that day,
that my guitar and diary are my friends tagging along,
not long, I'll be free of this privacy,
worshiping daily the trinity.

to never giving up, on writer's block.

People always ask me, why are you a writer? are you sad, terrified, scared, or in love? being a writer makes me feel alive, poetry gives me air to breathe, it gives me wings to fly and everything I do, it's related to you, poetry. poetry is that essence of walking down that empty space, with the head held high, it's that area I feel at home, and it's that time when I feel myself, because poetry makes me want to yearn for love. poetry makes me love, love myself, other people around me, because that's how poetry is. poetry is beautiful, natural and powerful, the most significant form of expression of emotions.

Being a writer isn't just a feeling, but the entire existence in the lap of words and the artistic nature of the most important feeling of being loved. poetry is magical, artists are magicians and writers, you my friends are life changers.
poetry is that one beautiful feeling in the world about me, myself and the words that feel like home.
for everything that has happened to me, and anything that is going to happen, writing is the constant feeling I've and everything that's connected to it. poetry is talking with the moon, and the words that weave magical thoughts, in this moonlight which pave the way for a mystical existence.

For you, a thousand times over

– Rae